Book Three

Step by Step
Piano Course

by

Edna Mae Burnam

To my first piano teacher—my mother.

PLAYBACK+
Speed • Pitch • Balance • Loop

The exclusive *Playback+* feature allows tempo changes without altering the pitch.
Loop points can also be set for repetition of tricky measures.

To access audio, visit:
www.halleonard.com/mylibrary

Enter Code
5815-0697-1298-8056

ISBN 978-1-4234-3607-2

Exclusively Distributed By

Visit Hal Leonard Online at
www.halleonard.com

World headquarters, contact:
Hal Leonard
7777 West Bluemound Road
Milwaukee, WI 53213
Email: info@halleonard.com

In Europe, contact:
Hal Leonard Europe Limited
42 Wigmore Street
Marylebone, London, W1U 2RY
Email: info@halleonardeurope.com

In Australia, contact:
Hal Leonard Australia Pty. Ltd.
4 Lentara Court
Cheltenham, Victoria, 3192 Australia
Email: info@halleonard.com.au

TO THE TEACHER

This is Book Three of EDNA MAE BURNAM'S PIANO COURSE—STEP BY STEP.

It is designed to follow her BOOK TWO by presenting new subjects in logical order and, ONE AT A TIME.

Sufficient work is given on each step so that the student will thoroughly comprehend it before going on to the next step.

Besides the explanatory remarks and the music that the student will learn to comprehend and play, this book, like BOOKS ONE and TWO, contains written work games and a final check-up. When the student completes this book, the following subjects will have been learned:—

1. To be able to name and play the following notes:—

2. Read and play:—

   Two-note chords
   Three-note chords
   A pick-up note

3. Learned the meaning of the following musical expression marks and to use them in playing:—

   f - loud - - - - - - (forte)
   mf - medium loud - - - (mezzo forte)
   ff - very loud - - - - - (fortissimo)
   p - soft - - - - - - (piano)
   mp - medium soft - - - (mezzo piano)
   pp - very soft - - - - - (pianissimo)
   $rit.$ - gradually slower - (ritard)

(continued)

4. Learned the meaning of the following musical signs and to use them in playing:—

accent = >

another sign for $\frac{4}{4}$ time = **C**

gradually louder =

gradually softer =

hold =

repeat =

staccato = •

first and second endings =

5. Play in the following keys:—
    C Major
    G Major
    D Major
    F Major

REPEAT SIGN

At the end of some pieces you will find a repeat sign.

Repeat
Sign

This means that you must play the piece a second time.

See the repeat sign at the end of LITTLE RIVER BOAT?

LITTLE RIVER BOAT

Lit - tle riv - er boat, Lit - tle riv - er boat, Chug, chug, chug-gin' a - long.

Lit - tle riv - er boat, Lit - tle riv - er boat, Chug, chug, chug-gin' a song.

A NEW TIME SIGNATURE

At the beginning of the piece below you will see the sign **C**

This means $\frac{4}{4}$ time.

Both time signatures below would be exactly alike in counting.

PRETTY LITTLE KITTY

Pret - ty lit - tle | Kit - ty,

Soft and | grey. Pret - ty lit - tle | Kit - ty, | Likes to | play.

THE HOLD SIGN

A sign like this ⌢ over a note or chord means

to **hold** the note or chord a **little longer.**

The piece below has some HOLD signs.

PLAYING STATUE

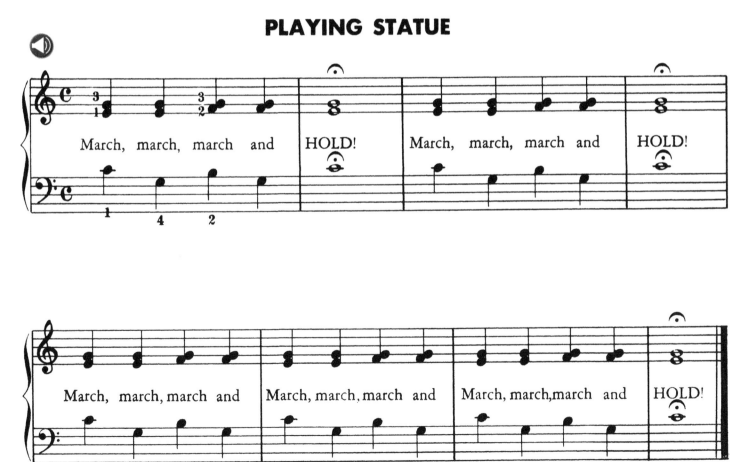

STACCATO SIGN

When you see a **dot above** a note—like this----➤ ♪   or **below** a note—like this⟍⟍ ♩

THESE NOTES ARE TO BE PLAYED STACCATO.

STACCATO means **short**—or **detached**.

STACCATO notes should be played with a **bouncing** touch—like a gentle **tap**.

Play the piece below with a **staccato** touch.

HAIL STONES

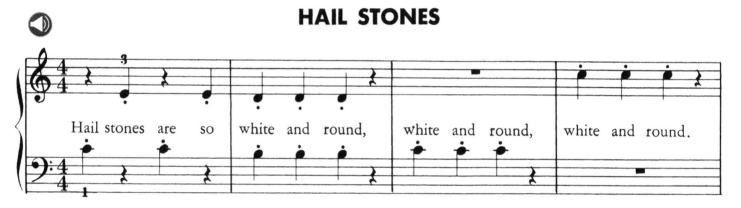

Hail stones are so white and round, white and round, white and round.

Hail stones bounce right off the ground, off the ground, off the ground.

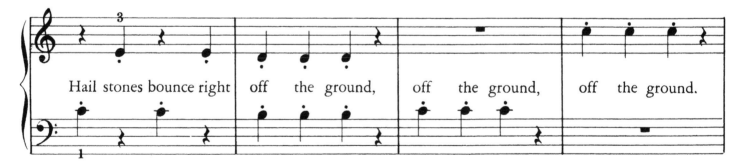

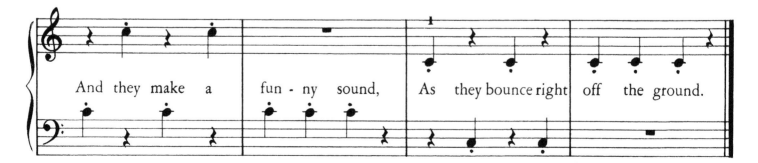

And they make a fun-ny sound, As they bounce right off the ground.

ACCENT SIGN

When you see a sign like this > above a note ♪ or notes ♫ it is an **accent** sign.

A note or chord with this sign above it should be played with **extra force.**

This piece has **accent** and **staccato** signs.

RAIN DANCE

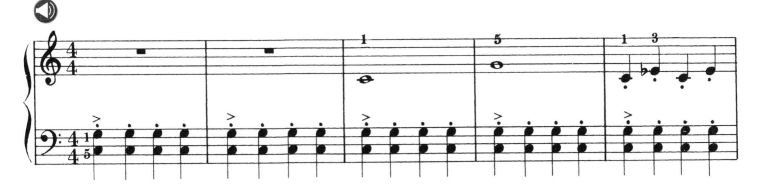

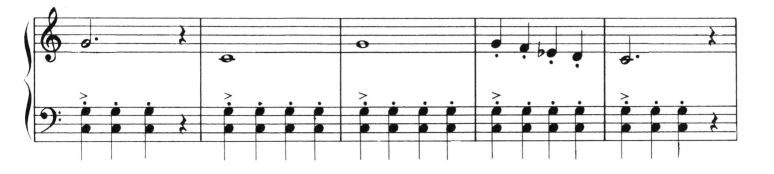

A NEW D

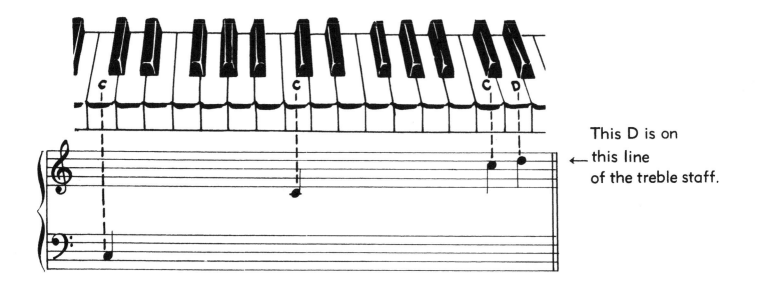

This D is on
← this line
of the treble staff.

FIRESIDE THOUGHTS

FIRST AND SECOND ENDING SIGNS

When you see a sign like this——————➔ at the end of a piece, it means the piece has **two endings**.

The **first** time, play through the **first ending only**—to the **repeat** sign.

Then go **back** to the **beginning** and **play** the piece **again**.

But this time do **NOT** play the **first ending** when you come to it. **Skip** it—and play the **second** ending.

POLKA DOTS

EXPRESSION MARKS

Here are some expression marks for you to learn.

mp - moderately soft - (mezzo piano)

p - soft - - - - - - - (piano)

pp - very soft - - - - (pianissimo)

mf - moderately loud - (mezzo forte)

f - loud - - - - - - - (forte)

ff - very loud - - - - (fortissimo)

A NEW E

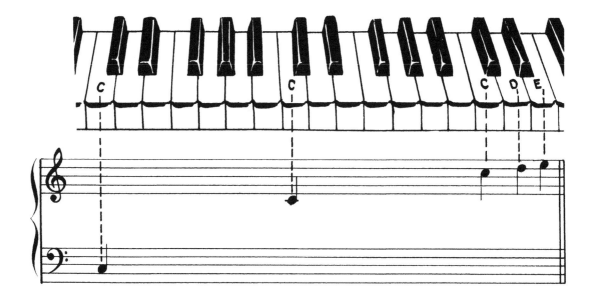

I HEAR AN ECHO

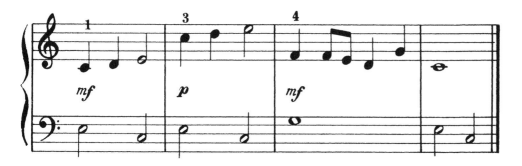

DOUBLE DECKER BUS

Fine

D.C. al fine

TRAINED SEALS

Each seal can juggle two balls.

Draw a line from each ball to the seal it matches.

You will find your cue written in the tail of each seal.

LIGHTHOUSES

Write the name of each note just **under** the note.

If you get every note right it means you were able to climb to the top of the lighthouse without

stumbling.

PEAS IN PODS

Each pod has peas in it.

How many peas are there in each pod?

There will be as many as there are counts in the notes.

Write how many counts in each pod in the leaf on the end of each pod.

A NEW F

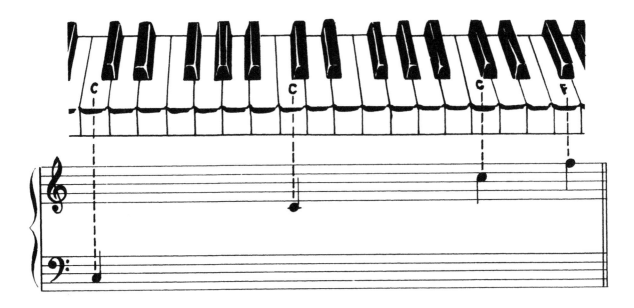

MERRY MIX-UP

MOUNTAIN CLIMBING

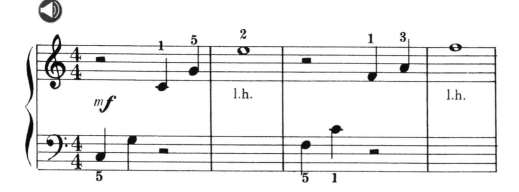

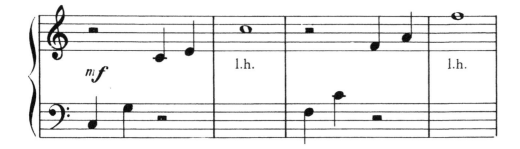

NEW EXPRESSION MARKS

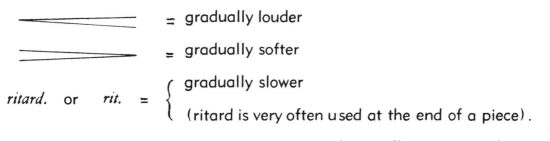

= gradually louder

= gradually softer

ritard. or *rit.* = { gradually slower

(ritard is very often used at the end of a piece).

The next piece contains a new expression mark as well as some you have used before.

TEN LITTLE DANCERS

Traditional

One lit-tle, Two lit-tle, | Three lit-tle danc-ers, | Four lit-tle, Five lit-tle, | Six lit-tle danc-ers,

Seven lit-tle, Eight lit-tle, | Nine lit-tle danc-ers, | Ten lit-tle danc-ers, *rit.* | spin!

A "PICK UP" COUNT

The piece "Sing a Song by the Campfire" is in $\frac{4}{4}$ time.

Are there **four** counts in the first measure? How many counts **do** you find?

This is the count just before the bar line, so it is the **last** count—or count **four.**

This is called a "pick up" count.

When you have a pick up count, always play the **first** count **after** the bar line with an **accent.**

This gives the "feel" of where the rhythm really begins.

Now look at the **last** measure of "Sing a Song by the Campfire".

Are there **four** counts in this measure? How many counts **do** you find?

There are only **three** counts in the last measure because we **began on count four in the first measure.**

SING A SONG BY THE CAMPFIRE

Sing a song by the camp-fire, Watch-ing the fire so bright.

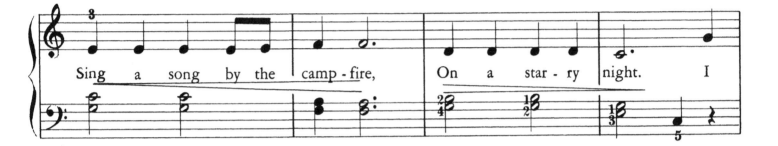

Sing a song by the camp-fire, On a star-ry night. I

like to sing a song by the camp-fire, On a star-ry night. I

like to sing a song by the camp-fire, When the stars are bright.

LEFT HAND PLAYS D TO THE RIGHT OF MIDDLE C

Play this note with the second finger of your left hand.

This note is **higher** than MIDDLE C so it must be D.

This is the way the D to the **right** of MIDDLE C is written when the **left** hand plays it.

Play these notes.

These notes are the **same** notes **on the keyboard**
but remember —

The **left** hand plays this one.

The **right** hand plays this one.

SAME NOTE

TIME FOR BED

LITTLE PAPOOSE, GOOD NIGHT

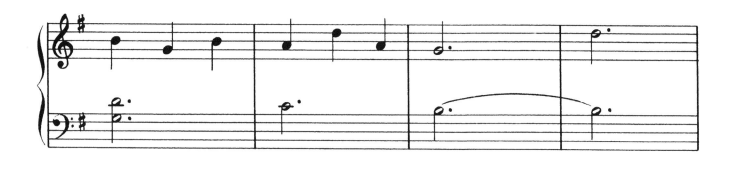

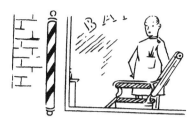

THE BARBER POLE

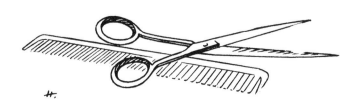

Play this note with the **second** finger of your **right** hand.

This note is **lower** than MIDDLE C, so it must be B.

This is the way the B to the **left** of MIDDLE C is written when the **right** hand plays it.

These notes are the **same** notes **on the keyboard** but remember —

The **left** hand plays this one.

The **right** hand plays this one.

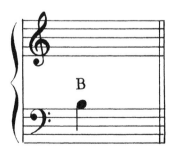

SAME NOTE

WALTZING AROUND

D. + 4. H.

SONG OF THE BEE

Fine

D.C. al fine

A NEW B

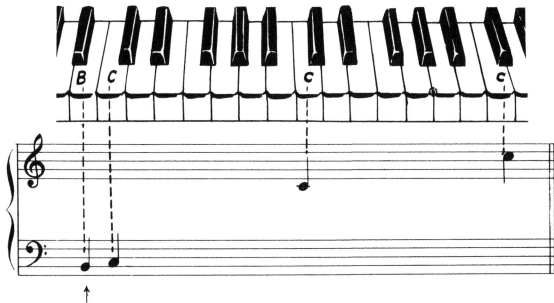

Here is another B

QUIET TIME

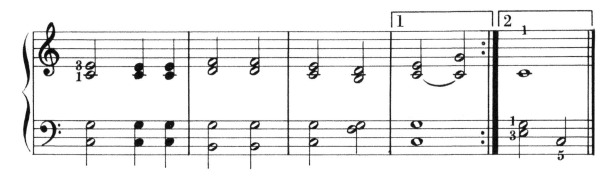

GRANDPA'S GLASSES

CUPS AND SAUCERS

Draw a line from each cup to the matching saucer.

HENS ON NESTS

Each hen is sitting on a nest. There are eggs in each nest. How many eggs are there in each nest? There are as many eggs as there are counts in the notes under the nest.

Write how many eggs in the nest over each hen.

Write the name of each note under the note.

If every one is correct, it means that the TV in that house is getting a clear picture.

A NEW A

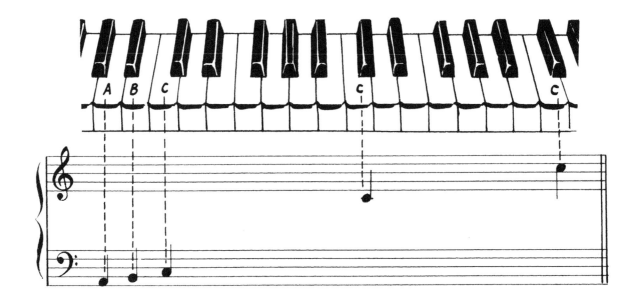

CURLEY CUES

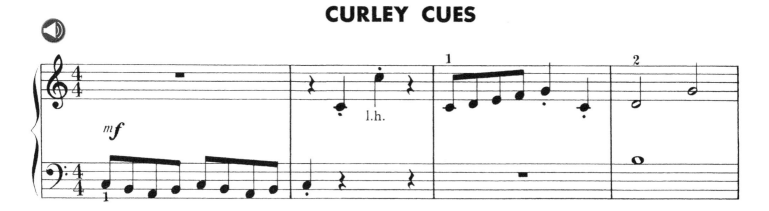

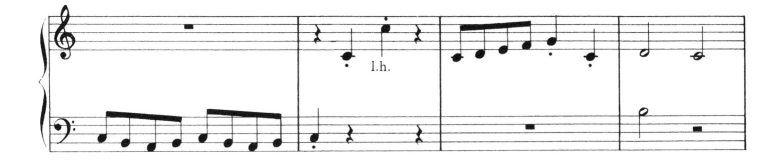

DRAGON CHANT

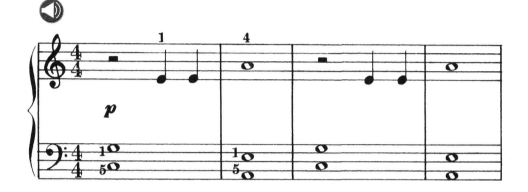

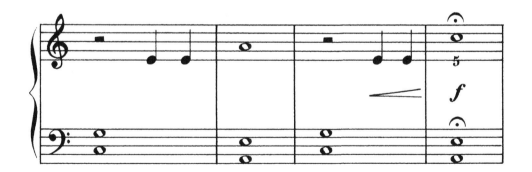

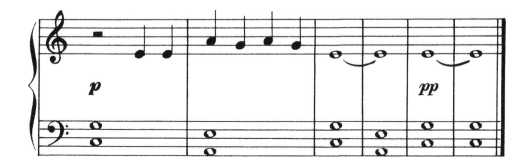

A NEW G

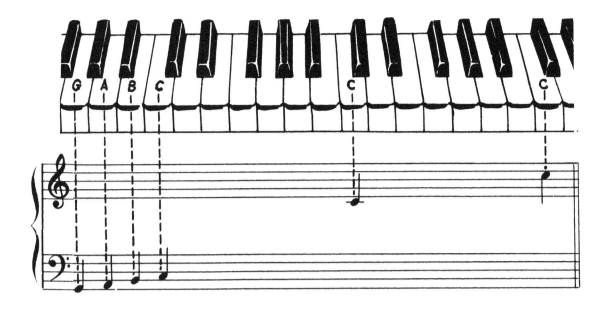

ACROBATS

CANDLELIGHT CHORALE

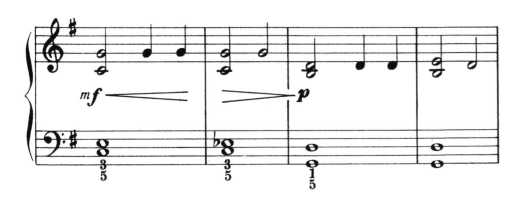

ON THE BANJO

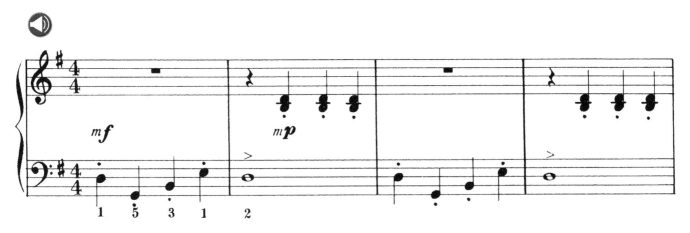

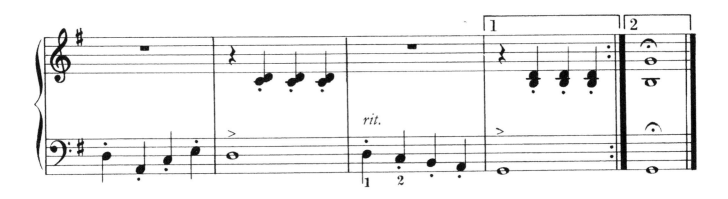

A THREE-NOTE CHORD

Here are three notes
played together.

This is a **three-note chord**
(or triad).

It is to be played with the
right hand using fingers
1, 3, 5.

Here is another **three-note chord.**

Play this with the **left hand** using fingers 5, 3, 1.

WALKING IN GALOSHES

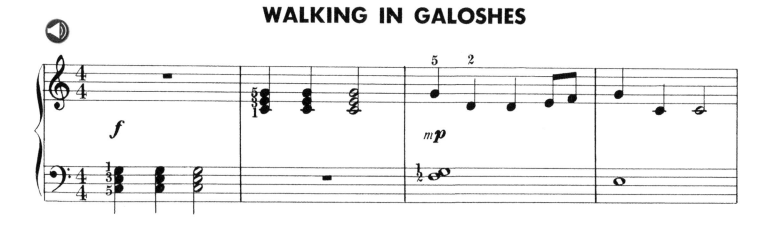

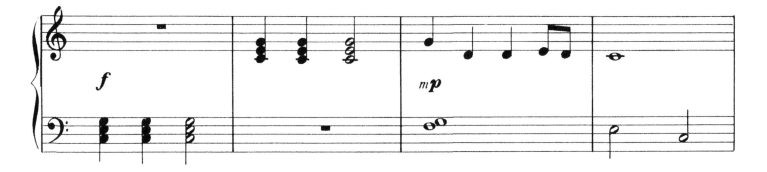

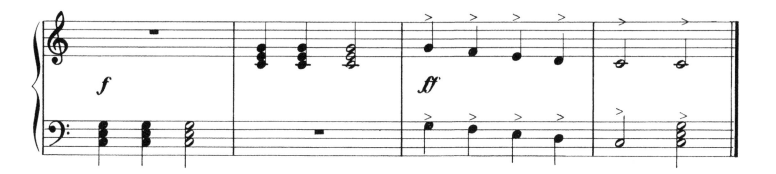

CHANGE OF KEY SIGNATURE

A piece does not **always** have the same key signature to the end of it.

Sometimes the key signature **changes.** Notice the key signature of this piece.

It **begins** in the **key of C major.** Then look at the key signature on the **third line.**

This part of the piece **is in F major.**

MARCHING HERE AND THERE

Fine

D.C. al fine

LITTLE ENGINES

Here are little engines. One is a **TREBLE ENGINE**—the other a **BASS ENGINE.**

Each engine must go to the next station, and each engineer wants to reach the next station without trouble.

There are notes on the train tracks (staffs). Write the name of each note under it.

If you get **every one right,** that engine reaches the end of the trip without trouble.
BE CAREFUL—so that each one will have a safe journey.

AIRPLANES

Each airplane has a different sign. The number of each plane is in the tailpiece.
Look at the numbers below to find the correct sign to draw in the wings of each plane.

Number 1 is done for you so you will know how to do the others.

1 - - - Treble clef

2 - - - Bass clef

3 - - - Accent

4 - - - Hold

5 - - - Sharp

6 - - - Flat

7 - - - Natural

8 - - - Staccato

9 - - - Very soft

10 - - - Gradually slower

11 - - - Very loud

12 - - - Four-count meter

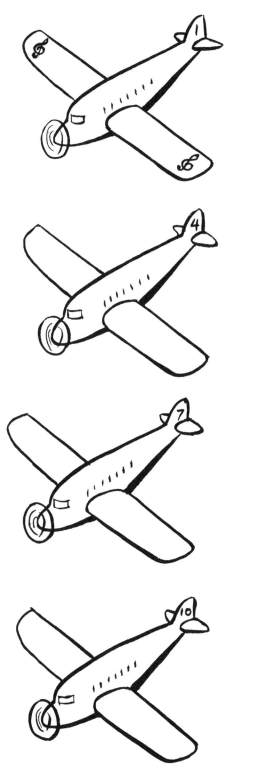

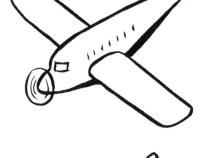

CLOCKS

Here are two clocks.

The top clock has **notes** in the **circles** that **equal counts one to twelve**—in order—just like the numbers on a regular clock. A quarter note gets one count.

Fill in the circles on the **lower** clock, making the **counts** in each circle the same as the clock above . . . **but change the kinds of notes.** (Circle one is finished for you).

You may put notes anywhere

in the circle—example:—

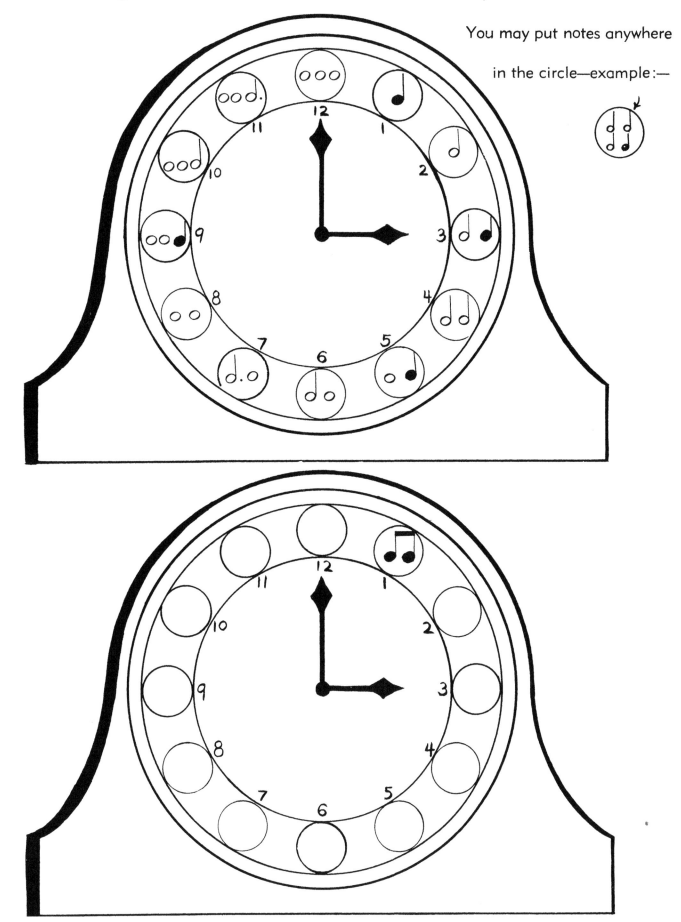

A NEW KEY SIGNATURE

Notice the key signature of this piece.

This is the **key of D major.**

The **two sharps to remember are F and C.**

BANJO ON MY KNEE

Stephen Foster
Arr. by E.M.B.

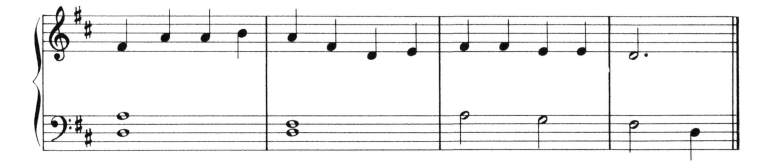

PUSSY WILLOW

FROM AN AIRPLANE WINDOW

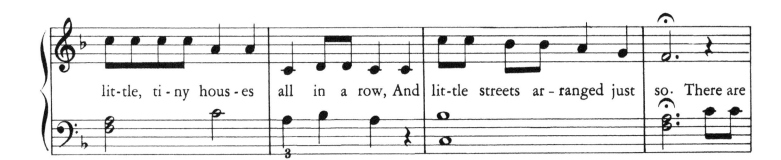

There's a lit-tle, ti-ny town 'way down there, Such a lit-tle, ti-ny town, from the air, With

little, ti-ny hous-es all in a row, And lit-tle streets ar-ranged just so. There are

lit-tle ti-ny peop-le go-ing to and fro, With lit-tle ti-ny hearts all a-glow, And

lit-tle, ti-ny cars that stop and go, In this lit-tle, ti-ny town be-low. There's a

lit-tle, ti-ny town 'way down there, Such a lit-tle ti-ny town from the air, with

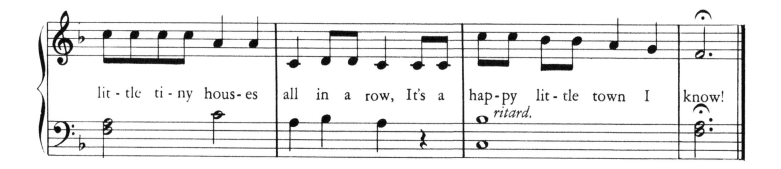

lit-tle ti-ny hous-es all in a row, It's a hap-py lit-tle town I know!

ritard.

THE WOODCHOPPER'S SONG

FINAL CHECK-UP

Your teacher will give you this final check-up.

Say aloud the names of the following notes:—

Show me an expression mark that means:—

Soft	*mf*
Loud	*p*
Medium soft	*pp*
Medium loud	*ff*
Very soft	*mp*
Very loud	*rit.*
Gradually slower	*f*

Show me a:—

    Three-note chord

    Two-note chord

    Pick-up note

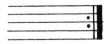

Show me a musical sign that means:—

    Accent

    $\frac{4}{4}$ time

    Hold

    First and second ending

    Staccato

    Gradually softer

    Repeat

    Gradually louder

    C Major

    G Major

Show me the key signature for:—   D Major

    F Major

Certificate of Merit

This certifies that

....

has successfully completed

BOOK THREE
OF
EDNA MAE BURNAM'S
PIANO COURSE

STEP BY STEP

and is eligible for promotion to

BOOK FOUR

.... Teacher

Date..

Edna Mae Burnam was a pioneer in piano publishing. The creator of the iconic *A Dozen a Day* technique series and *Step by Step* method was born on September 15, 1907 in Sacramento, California. She began lessons with her mother, a piano teacher who drove a horse and buggy daily through the Sutter Buttes mountain range to reach her students. In college Burnam decided that she too enjoyed teaching young children, and majored in elementary education at California State University (then Chico State College) with a minor in music. She spent several years teaching kindergarten in public schools before starting her own piano studio and raising daughters Pat and Peggy. She delighted in composing for her students, and took theory and harmony lessons from her husband David (a music professor and conductor of the Sacramento Symphony in the 1940s).

Burnam began submitting original pieces to publishers in the mid-1930s, and was thrilled when one of them, "The Clock That Stopped," was accepted, even though her remuneration was a mere $20. Undaunted, the industrious composer sent in the first *A Dozen a Day* manuscript to her Willis editor in 1950, complete with stick-figure sketches for each exercise. Her editor loved the simple genius of the playful artwork resembling a musical technique, and so did students and teachers: the book rapidly blossomed into a series of seven and continues to sell millions of copies. In 1959, the first book in the *Step by Step* series was published, with hundreds of individual songs and pieces along the way, often identified by whimsical titles in Burnam's trademark style.

The immense popularity of her books solidified Edna Mae Burnam's place and reputation in music publishing history, yet throughout her lifetime she remained humble and effervescent. "I always left our conversations feeling upbeat and happy," says Kevin Cranley, Willis president. "She could charm the legs off a piano bench," Bob Sylva of the *Sacramento Bee* wrote, "make a melody out of a soap bubble, and a song out of a moon beam."

Burnam died in 2007, a few months shy of her 100th birthday. "Music enriches anybody's life, even if you don't turn out to be musical," she said once in an interview. "I can't imagine being in a house without a piano."

A DOZEN A DAY

by Edna Mae Burnam

The **A Dozen A Day** books are universally recognized as one of the most remarkable technique series on the market for all ages! Each book in this series contains short warm-up exercises to be played at the beginning of each practice session, providing excellent day-to-day training for the student. All book/audio versions include orchestrated accompaniments by Ric Ianonne.

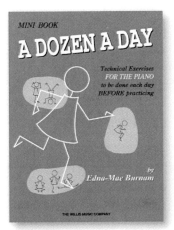

MINI BOOK
00404073 Book Only $6.99
00406472 Book/Audio $10.99

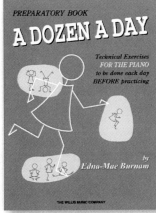

PREPARATORY BOOK
00414222 Book Only $6.99
00406476 Book/Audio $10.99

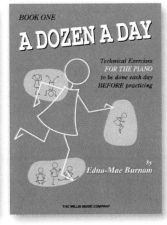

BOOK 1
00413366 Book Only $6.99
00406481 Book/Audio $10.99

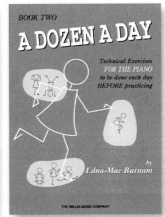

BOOK 2
00413826 Book Only $6.99
00406485 Book/Audio $10.99

BOOK 3
00414136 Book Only $7.99
00416760 Book/Audio $10.99

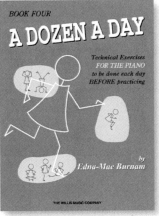

BOOK 4
00415686 Book Only $7.99
00416761 Book/Audio $11.99

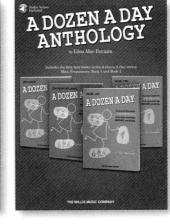

**PLAY WITH EASE
IN MANY KEYS**
00416395 Book Only $6.99

**A DOZEN A DAY
ANTHOLOGY**
00158307 Book/Audio $25.99

ALSO AVAILABLE:
The **A Dozen A Day Songbook** series containing Broadway, movie, and pop hits!

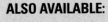

Visit Hal Leonard Online at **www.halleonard.com**

WILLIS MUSIC

EXCLUSIVELY DISTRIBUTED BY

HAL•LEONARD®

Prices, contents, and availability subject to change without notice. Prices listed in U.S. funds.